THE WHO

THE FAREWELL TOUR

CHICAGO

THE WHO

The Farewell Tour

Photographs by Philip Kamin
Text by Peter Goddard

SIDGWICK & JACKSON
LONDON

First published in Great Britain in 1983 by Sidgwick & Jackson Ltd.
Originally published in Canada in 1983 by General Publishing Co. Limited

ISBN 0-283-98979-3

Printed in Canada for
Sidgwick & Jackson Ltd.
1 Tavistock Chambers
Bloomsbury Way
London WC1A 2SG

Text design by **Joe Stevens Graphic Design**

Acknowledgments

For Pearl, Sam, Bernie.

Very special thanks to The Who, Mason Buck, Paul Wasserman, Chris Chappel, and Bob Bender.

Thanks also to my assistant Bruce Evans, Robert Bonneville, my assistant on tour, Cathy Spanton for travel arrangements, and Evelyn Watt.

I would also like to thank Allan Stokell, C.J. Morgan and Don Hood at Positive Images, Toronto; Doug Paddey, Marty Ingles and Gary Beck at Canon Cameras of Canada; Steve Coomber at Ilford Films; Bob, Glen and Skip at Steichenlab, Toronto.

P.K.

To Kate, that *who*.

Thanks to Mason Buck, and David Pritchard and Alan Lysaght at Sonic Workshop, Toronto.

P.G.

Chapter I

PHILADELPHIA

As the van thumps and lurches up the ramp leading from the arena, the talk turns to baseball.

Would the Dodgers make it into the World Series? Would San Diego? Might there be a "freeway series"?

It takes mere minutes to leave the vast parking lot around the Capitol Center in Largo, Maryland and we head back to our various hotel rooms in downtown Washington. Limos slip by us, sleek in the night, but no one pays much attention. Instead, it's the slumping Yankees, the Phillies, the Expos. Hey, how about the White Sox? Improved. Lotsa potential.

A curious group this, at least when it comes to baseball talk. It's not the sports media but the *rock* media. Out just ahead on the pot-holed highway is Pete Hamill, working on a piece for *New York* magazine. Inside the van itself is writer Kurt Loder, beginning a cover piece for *Rolling Stone*. Up front a chatty Toronto rock columnist talks to a feature writer from Chicago. And right in the middle of it all is, energy unflagging as always, Lisa Robinson, from the *New York Post*.

We're all here for the same reason — the first show of The Who's last tour — but no one really has much to say about it, at least not here, not now. Of course it's because everyone's still sorting it out, I figure. But there's more to it than that.

But what? This is The Who's last tour, isn't it? The last harrah by one of the great bands? Waiting for a light to change, I check my notes from the concert in the garish light thrown by the sign of a grotty little bar on the corner:

BUFFALO

"Amazing. *Twist and Shout* last piece. By Entwistle. He has best rock voice of the lot. He doesn't want to quit... muscles on Kenney Jones's arms...*Eminence Front,* great...*Baba O'Riley, Won't Get Fooled Again, Behind Blue Eyes*...Daltrey distracted. Townshend's odd smile. Ask him...."

The van slides into the dark and in only a few moments we're at the Dolly Madison Hotel, the band's digs for the next few days and command center for the press. Long gone are the days of battered TV sets hurtling out of wrecked hotel rooms. Now it's the small, *right* hotel and rooms with period furniture. It's an early night. The parties will come later in the tour.

WASHINGTON, D.C.

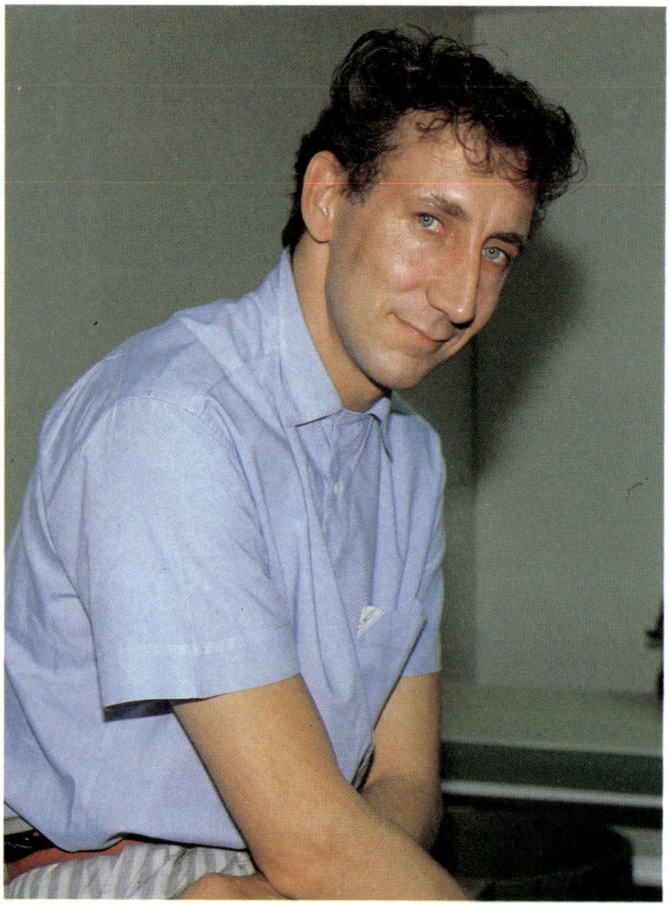

NEW YORK

NEW YORK

The beginning of the end began in private, relatively speaking — at the rehearsal, not the concert. The concert itself produced the format which would hold for the most part throughout both legs of the tour. It was long. It was loud. And it was vintage Who; that kind of prolonged musical explosion which, love it or hate it, is awesome in its way.

It's also impenetrable in another way, this Who performance. It's a fixed quantity, refinement on a refinement on a refinement, with few rough edges of excess. There's no dramatic shape here but one continuous beam of intensity. Unvarying. Laser-pure. A magic horizon of sound.

It's dramatic, but in a curious way it's not theatrical. It allows description, but not explanation.

But the rehearsal was different. There was an unhurried, unruffled tone about it. No one pressed. Everyone was milling about. And from this calm beginning we could see the momentum gathering. A camera crew shooting ads for Schlitz Beer, sponsors of the tour, crowded around the front of the stage as the

WASHINGTON, D.C.

band began to warm up. Bob Bender, the one-time Olympic wrestler who has guarded The Who during recent tours, smiled as he saw some familiar faces while he ambled about.

Kenney Jones, looking far more relaxed than he did on the band's last tour — the first since he replaced Keith Moon — seemed to be actually enjoying himself. "There was so much pressure the last time," he told me off-handedly, during a break. "Roger kept trying to explain my presence, but it always came out wrong." Well, maybe. What Daltrey had been saying was that Jones could never replace Moon. "But now the pressure's off," the drummer went on.

The break over, the band launched into *Won't Get Fooled Again* and a couple of other vintage pieces for the Schlitz crew when, abruptly and for no apparent reason — the

WASHINGTON, D.C.

WASHINGTON, D.C.

filming was over — The Who went into overdrive.

There was Townshend whipping down his hand in one mighty, back-alley round-house swing that is so powerful a guitar string slashes through the flesh on his hand. And there was Daltrey letting out a shriek that had a sound engineer wincing. And it was all thunder and pounding and wonderful Who stuff and damn if they couldn't stop it.

Terrific. The momentum took over. It wouldn't let go. The camera crew was packing up, most of the shooting was finished, but there's Townshend leaping about like mad, his

TORONTO

PREVIOUS SPREAD
TORONTO

WASHINGTON, D.C.

arm whirling and the craziest, happiest, gooniest smile on his face, trying to drop the ultimately heavy chord to anchor this whole thing...and, as in Beethoven, each final thump demands that a bigger one comes next.

And the weirdest thing happened. Everyone ended up staring, all gee-whiz and slack-jawed. Everyone was listening too, of course — although after hearing an hour or so of The Who in rehearsal one becomes blasé to any chunk of raw sound this side of the crash of a Boeing 747 — but no one was really *hearing*.

What was going on went beyond sound, however extreme. The Who, it seemed, had finally started something they could not stop. It was out of hand...well, until Townshend just about knocked himself senseless and finally whomped out one gigantic, final, teeth-chattering chord. *Wrangggg!*

Dead silence. Everyone still stared at the stage. "We know how to start something," he said with a wry, thin smile. "It's stopping we have trouble with."

Chapter 2

They've always been the band of the grand, emotional gesture. The Mod's band. The Pop Art Band. Bang! Pow! Zap! Union Jack shirts and Keith Moon's bull's-eye T-shirt. It's been Townshend in full flight, his arms slamming down on his guitar after one great windmill sweep; it's been Daltrey whirling his microphone around his head like some sort of electronic lariat.

And now The Who's making the grandest emotional gesture of all. It's quitting the road after eighteen years — and quitting after Daltrey had thought they never would.

"We're finished and I'm glad," the singer had said early on in the tour. "We're all glad, I think. Now that we don't have to worry about being The Who we can get on to new projects. We'll still work together; I can't imagine not working with Pete Townshend. We just won't be The Who."

How they're ending it is one matter — a tour taking in forty cities and ending with a final Pay TV special from Toronto. Actually, the clean-cut final concert we had heard about at first grew a mite ambiguous by the time the band arrived exhausted in Toronto in mid-December, waiting for the TV crews to show up.

TORONTO

PHILADELPHIA

All the touring wasn't exactly going to end in Canada, we began to find out. A mini-Australian tour was in the works. European gigs were planned. Future albums could be expected. By the end of it all we'd come to realize it wasn't the complete end at all.

Still, quitting the road is a signal for change for any rock band. It meant losing *live* contact with your audience. The Who were severing some crucial ties. So this story seemed ready-made — another rock band was packing it in and this time it was one of the big ones. Even the subtext was ready-made — Pete Townshend's booze and pills binges in recent years had been the final straw.

The faith had been broken — Townshend's faith in himself, his faith in the band, and, ultimately, the faith Daltrey had in him.

BUFFALO

PHILADELPHIA

Why they were ending it now became another matter entirely, though. The way Roger saw it, the band's style had come from Moon but it remained "an extension" of Pete's work. But he, Roger, was still very much at the heart of it all. He'd been its first leader. He still planned the shows and felt no one else could do it as well as he did. In essence, he was still at least the *co*-leader by virtue of his belief in The Who. When this belief was shattered, so was The Who itself.

For Daltrey and Townshend, the life-long friends who "can't stay in the same room together," as Daltrey puts it, The Who had become entirely a personal matter. So quitting the road was a personal matter, too. Pete wants out; Roger wants out, too.

Good story. But it doesn't end there. Questions must be asked. And what exactly is ending is the most perplexing one of all. What has The Who meant to rock? Beyond all the givens of the story lays the real problem. The Who *are not explained*.

Who are The Who after all?

For all the publicity that's come their way — after eleven fans were asphyxiated before a 1979 concert in Cincinnati's Riverfront Coliseum, they became front-page news — they're still rock's best-kept big secret.

Not that they haven't gone public before. Townshend's guitar-smashing finales were one of the '60s most memorable images; *Tommy* was rock's first full-scale work; their two movies, "Quadrophenia" and "The Kids Are All Right," are, in fact, histories of the kind of England the band grew up in; and when Keith Moon, their brilliant, maniacal hard-living drummer, died in 1978 of what was described as a "vast overdose" of pills, rock — used to suicidal behavior, vast indulgences and inevitable death by then — was nonetheless shocked.

Yet of all the major-league acts in rock, The Rolling Stones, The Beatles, David Bowie, Jim Morrison, The Clash included, The Who have never fully gone public. Despite better books being written on them than are accorded most bands, The Who remain something of a secret. They're a secret to those who really do know rock and something of a mystery to those who do not.

It has in part to do with identity. They're one kind of band in the Midwest — it's good old Pete & heavy metal & all that rousing stuff. They're another kind on the east coast — very British & intellectual even. They're one band in Canada and entirely something else in England and Europe. You can rightfully think you understand The Stones to some degree (even if indeed it's only Mick Jagger you're hooked on) and not care much about rock music. The same can be said about The Beatles or Bob Dylan or Elvis Costello or Fleetwood Mac or David Bowie. But it doesn't really work with The Who.

And there's an irony here. It's almost as if all of Townshend's lavish and intelligent explanations have acted as a smokescreen. Rather than clarifying the what's and why's of The Who, they've only proven to make the issues seem more distant. The point is, listen to The Who and you pick up blips directly from the central nervous system of rock.

They're rock without apologies or explanation. They're the inside job, the proof of rock's original hard-headed intentions; proof that it would never be completely accommodating. As long as The Who have been there, living dangerously close to the edge, rock would never be completely part of the mainstream.

They are, to broaden the argument the way

TORONTO *WASHINGTON, D.C.*

TORONTO

WASHINGTON, D.C.

Townshend himself likes to do, the '60s *without* apologies — older, crustier, louder, brighter. *My Generation* is exactly that to Townshend — it's *his* generation still alive and kicking. Everywhere else the '60s generation has made accommodations: it's cut its hair and it made its peace over the Viet Nam war. Its radicals are now on the lecture circuit, its rebels are writing their memoirs. Jane Fonda's the author of two exercise books; her husband, Tom Hayden, one of the Chicago Seven, is a member of the state legislature of California.

We've forgiven our parents, they've forgiven us, and everything's alright — or so we pretend to think. But the baby boom has lots of unfinished business. Certainly Townshend's no longer the pouty kid with the big honker. He hobnobs with the titled and rich. He's not about to apologize for his money or his status. But unlike many others, he hasn't completely forgotten what he started out to prove.

It's personal. He says his success at kicking his alcoholism — "up almost to a bottle and a half of brandy a day, neat" — left him with a new challenge: "Change, radical change, for me. If I could leave all the booze and drugs behind, I could leave this behind, too."

It's personal for Daltrey, too — deeply

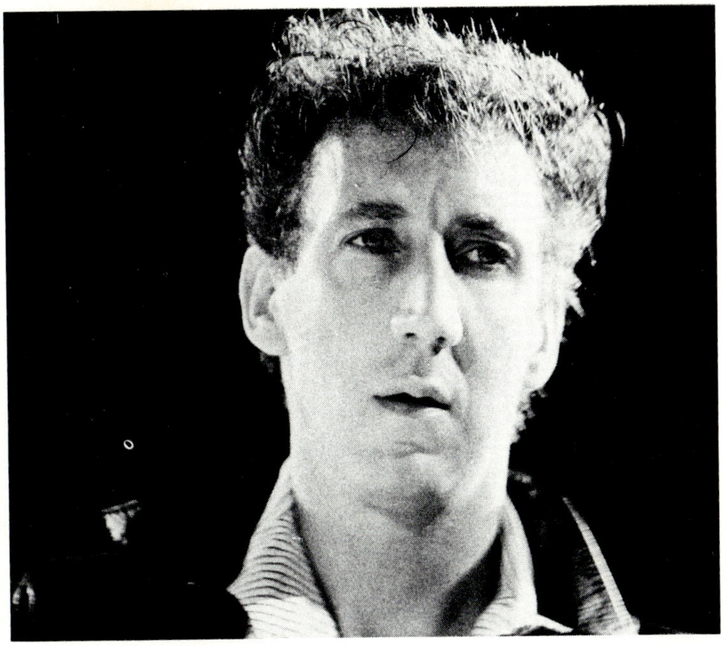

NEW YORK

TORONTO

TORONTO

personal. He says he believed in the band and all that it could accomplish up until its chief creative force, Pete Townshend, started to kill himself two years ago.

"That ended it all for me," he adds, his eyes clouding over. "I was hurt. I thought we were the best rock band in the world till then. I thought we could change the world until then. What Pete did proved we couldn't."

We were talking in Washington merely hours before they went out to work for the first time in two years.

"A lot of people in the group and a lot of

WASHINGTON, D.C.

PHILADELPHIA

WASHINGTON, D.C.

BUFFALO

PHILADELPHIA

ABOVE
PHILADELPHIA

PHILADELPHIA

PHILADELPHIA

ABOVE
PHILADELPHIA

WASHINGTON, D.C.

WASHINGTON, D.C.

people around the group don't want to admit this is happening, but this is the end of The Who," Townshend explains — although as Roger would indicate later, nothing should ever be considered that final. The two would be contradicting each other throughout the tour.

"They may not be as ready to make that radical change in their life, but that's tough. I've come too close to death, to really dying, to fool around anymore. I want control of my life and I'm not in control of it in this band."

The hotel suite we were in looked like an ambassador's apartment. The Japanese print on the wall seemed real; the furniture antique. Yet nothing on earth would have made him fit in here. Something of the early '60s London Mod was still about him. He'll never shake it.

He had been up early — something that's easier to do since he's not drinking. He sipped some coffee: "I used to think I could control everything, even the press. But now I know I can't. I'm just going to be honest. I was having

PHILADELPHIA

NEW YORK

HICAGO

dinner with David Bowie not long ago and he was saying how he had to watch everything he did, or 'they would misquote him.' He always worried that 'they' wouldn't understand. Well, I don't know who he means by 'them.' I do know that if you tell the truth, and only half of it is printed, at least that's something. It's odd. Bowie gave me his phone number but when I called it a month later, he had changed it.

"The reason The Who has had such good press for so long is that we've been good copy — we've been both articulate and sensational. The Who is a better example of a rock'n'roll band than The Rolling Stones because we are more diverse while also being more ordinary. We are not the glamorous, dangerous figures that The Stones are. In the past we attempted to look that way, to look rebellious, but that wasn't us. Even Keith Moon — he wouldn't have pulled a knife on anybody.

"But we've been trapped too long by what we've been. We've needed to change."

YAMAHA
YAMAHA

NEW YORK

OUISVILLE

BUFFALO

Chapter 3

En route to the concert.

I see Jacquie must have made it to the concert.

As long as the weather holds out, Jacquie walks the triangle in front of the Continental Hotel, on Thomas Circle, downtown Washington D.C. She takes it slowly and if all goes well she never makes it all the way around.

You'll see her, a ripple of pink and white, meander up Vermont Avenue. Pause. Walk, pause. Walk, then…

Well, looking down from your window in the Continental, you might see a car pull over to the curb. For what? To ask directions from the girl in the ultra-pink short-shorts and see-through blouse? Why, of course. Isn't that what she always tells the cops? Helpful as always to the bemused and bewildered, she always gets in to show the driver the way. Often it's around the world.

An hour or so later, she's usually back. But not tonight, I notice as I glance out my hotel room window. Some of the others are there, with umbrellas in case it rains. But not her. And I'm wondering if she did what she promised.

We'd met by design — her's, not mine. Jacquie had found out where The Who were

BUFFALO

BUFFALO

staying before The Who themselves did. And being an enormous Who fan, she figured she had to get seats to the show. Like desperate, you know?

In the old days it was relatively simple, she told me. All you needed was to meet someone in the crew who'd been out on the road too long and who was relatively nice. Thereafter would follow a simple exchange of services. He'd be a happier man and she'd be in possession of a pass of some sort, either a friend-of-group pass or backstage or something.

But it didn't work out this time. "There's too much organization here, you know?" she complained when we met in the lobby of the Dolly Madison and I recognized her from her old haunt. "Even the crew has crew and they've all got wives and lawyers and... hey, do you have...?"

Alas, I told her, I had nothing. I'm stuck in vans and carted around. "Okay," she shrugged. "But you know? If I do get in, you know for old

BUFFALO

WASHINGTON, D.C.

time's sake, I'm gonna show 'em my tattoo. I had it put on in London, England. In Carnaby Street, you know."

She gave me a peek. Nice. There, just about at the curve of her right buttock I saw the beginning of a rosy Union Jack. I'm not sentimental usually, but I could see how the band might like to see it — for old time's sake.

Mick Jagger and daughter Jade showed up at the band's show in Philadelphia and Bruce Springsteen caught up with them in Phoenix and Cleveland, where the American portion of the tour ended. But unlike The Rolling Stones' last cross-continent tour, The Who's generally didn't gather many celebrities as they rolled.

The first night had set the tone. Joan Jett was backstage, but she seemed merely to be part of the crowd. Just another fan. This crowd was distinctly business-like. The Stones had been represented alright by Art Collins,

from their New York office. There were radio biggies and agency biggies and promoters. And as John Entwistle, the taciturn bassist who really will miss touring, has said, money-making wasn't far from The Who's minds either when this tour was planned.

Who's generation is this anyway? The Stones' audience had included everyone from every generation who knew his way to a radio dial. No single age group was dominant.

That wasn't the case with The Who. This was a younger crowd (as it would prove to be throughout the tour). For every person at the Capitol Center out of nostalgia, there were dozens who'd come simply to be buzzed. If nothing else, what was being proven was that after eighteen years, and a number of admittedly weak albums, The Who were still competitive.

LOUISVILLE

PREVIOUS SPREAD
WASHINGTON, D.C.

LOUISVILLE

WASHINGTON, D.C.

NEW YORK

David Johansen opened the show, trying hard — maybe too hard. A number of acts opened for the band: John Cougar, Joe Jackson, T-Bone Burnett, The Rockets, and The Clash ("my favorite band of the moment," explained Pete at one press conference). Some were out-selling The Who in terms of records, some were younger and hipper. But it always remained a Who show.

Joan Jett. Sitting on a tin drum. One of the hottest acts in rock at the time, she was all dark-eyed and profoundly icy until Townshend came over to talk to her.

As I watch them, I realize that his own daughter Emma, who has a group in London,

the Launderettes, is not much younger than Joan Jett. Suddenly Jett, despite the hard black makeup, seemed even younger. She swung her legs casually, the way a kid might. She seemed nervous. She told him, "this is my birthday," looking soft and smiling and utterly enthralled by him.

The singer on stage had a baby beer belly hanging over his tight pink pants. What's this age thing The Who were worrying about? By 8:25 P.M. the demand from the crowd was gripping the mood like a fist.

It wouldn't relent. "I can't tell you what I would've done if I couldn't get to this," said Ronnie. He'd just made it up from Baltimore with plans of seeing both Washington shows. The girl with him seemed totally terrified just by the crowd. "Since I first heard them I've not listened to any other band. I don't wanna know about any other band."

He was a skinny guy with his sleeves rolled up high and tight above his elbows. His thin muscles were tensed. His girl took one look at his clenched fists and white knuckles and stared even more intently at the stage.

NEW YORK

PREVIOUS PAGE
CHICAGO

WASHINGTON, D.C.

NEW YORK

I headed back into the crowd.

"When we really get going, we've always had the sense that we were pushing the stage out towards the audience," Townshend had been telling me. Well, from the top they pushed hard.

They opened with *Substitute*, as clear and hard as a slice of metal and the intensity was unrelenting from the beginning — unlike the opening of the last tour in New York three years before when things sagged from the very start. It was, perhaps, that everyone — including the band itself — had known Moon was missing. Perhaps it was because Townshend was beginning to wreck himself. For whatever reason, the show had missed in some intangible way. And when The Who are ever so slightly off, it is in fact glaring.

But in Washington, you could hear a new muscularity in Kenney Jones's drumming in *I Can't Explain*. Some of the riffs in other pieces were reminiscent of Moon, but this was definitely a different style of work. The rest of the band had altered its style to accommodate and Townshend was stretching out more in his solos.

Eminence Front, with its slowly gathering power punch, was followed by *Cry If You Want, Baba O'Riley* and *Won't Get Fooled Again. Magic Bus,* with an arcing, nicely shaped Townshend solo, began the encore.

I'd made it back to the topmost seats to find a phone when suddenly an enormous yelling match starts near by. Richard Harrington, rock critic for *The Washington Post*, had dashed back to the press room to file his review and was being stopped by a guard.

Nothing Harrington could say would change the guard's mind. They leaned angrily towards each other. If push were to come to shove I'd place my final bets on Harrington getting to his phone — he's solidly built and seemed a good yeller — but the guard hung in there.

Down the hall, another scuffle had broken out. Two kids caught fighting in their seats were in the process of being ejected by three enormous guards. Any one of the guards out-weighed both of the kids. But, like Harrington, the fans weren't going to go easily.

"WHAT DO YA MEAN KICK US OUT?" one screamed.

"MAN, THIS IS A WHO CONCERT," the other yelled. "THAT WASN'T FIGHTING. THAT WAS JUST FOOLING AROUND."

They disappeared around another door. So had Harrington. Apparently, he'd made it to the press room. At least there'd been one small victory.

I hurried back to get nearer the stage just in time to hear the band catch everyone by surprise, finishing with *Twist and Shout*. Entwistle sings it as raucously as possible and it works.

The roar back from the crowd is deafening and — there! right! — amid all the flutter Union Jacks, those hand-made and those bought from the band's concessions, was a distinctly curvy one. A tattoo.

Jacquie.

The next morning I read Harrington's review in the *Post* — the band "performed with the vivid urgency of beginners... openly celebrating their history."

"When we really get going, we've always had the sense that we were pushing the stage out towards the audience," echoes back to me. The show had been one great push from beginning to end.

WASHINGTON, D.C.

Chapter 4

"That was one of the problems with us," Roger Daltrey tells me one afternoon. It's still early in the tour and he's sorting out what it means. By the end, as he'll tell Bruce Springsteen one night, he's exhausted.

"Pete forgot he was writing about his generation — *our* generation. When that happened we started to be about something else. It's not a question of playing, exactly. I think we're playing better than we ever have been. It's a question of belief. I used to believe in this band in a way I don't now. I really, really used to believe The Who could change the world. I don't think we can anymore."

The Who have long been obsessed with history — not just their own, but as *My Generation* says, with their generation's. They grew up near each other in the Shepherd's Bush, Chiswick, Wembley section of London and they knew many of the same people and listened to many of the same records.

And maybe this is what sets them apart from guys who ended up in other bands — this common sense of place and mutual friends.

BUFFALO *LOUISVILLE*

WASHINGTON, D.C.

PREVIOUS PAGE
CHICAGO

Rarely has there been a band as fractious as this one, Daltrey, Moon and Townshend, each having thumped one another at one time or another. Rarely has one had individuals who've needed each other as much. (Townshend has marvelled how everyone let him evolve *Tommy* the slow and often hesitant way he did.)

Music was the main link between Keith Richards and Mick Jagger, at first anyhow. The link in the Small Faces was style: they were all Mods. Like The Beatles, who sorted through various personnel before arriving at the final lineup, Townshend, Entwistle and Daltrey were together in a closer way, in a way kids from the same neighborhood are always together. They liked the same stuff.

This is no small matter, especially these days as the tour travels on, with Roger saying that he and Pete really have nothing much to say to one another and John thinking he might quit the band flat if it *doesn't* tour. Still feuding after all these years, but...

As they all know, they can't escape from each other for a dozen different reasons. What they have in common is a sense of what The Who was supposed to mean — to themselves and to everyone else. Townshend was proud of *My Generation* when he wrote it. He feels something special about *Tommy*. What thrilled him was the way he was able to reach such a huge audience through *Tommy*, how it managed speak to Who fans and foes alike.

It was exactly the kind of larger-than-life gesture everyone understood at the time. The Who grew up at the center of the baby boom, the largest single generation in history to be so obsessed with itself. And while the generation itself has fragmented and fragmented again, much of this self-obsession has not.

CHICAGO

This was a generation which felt it could create its own history. And while The Who are about a little bit of everything (like the best bands in rock), threaded through all their work is something unique — this ongoing review of its own history.

And at this moment, Daltrey is thinking about just that. He stares down at his hands and chooses every word carefully. But here's a most curious thing. He's all bright and blue-eyed and sunny: he's tanned and muscular from all his running and massages and workouts, his teeth straight out of a toothpaste commercial. He is as open as a clear day to look at him. But his voice is all shadows and mysteries. It sits way down his throat, a little round, hooded sound. He can cut a word in two just by a swallow.

I'd been ready for someone who was shy; I'd heard lots about his reputation as a brawler and felt that the opposite was just as likely to be true, that here was the heart of the band, the one who had all the feeling, who was its moral center. I wasn't ready for someone who wore his feelings so close to the surface.

Townshend marvels at the way audiences, particularly the women, react to Roger: "They think it's all so difficult. They'll come back-stage and say to him, 'You're so healthy, you ran on the stage throughout the entire song.' Well, when he goes off running in the morning he's gone for about four hours, swinging from tree to tree, lamp to lamp, whatever. He plays a couple of hours of squash, lifts a load of weights. And they think thirty seconds of jogging on the spot is dazzling. But that's The Who all over. Nothing has ever come easily, naturally. We were never a natural team. We've never understood why we've worked together so well."

Roger was born March 1, 1944. He had great report cards from school early on but was eventually thrown out because of smoking. He's often said that finding The Who probably was the major factor that kept him out of jail. Maybe so, but he never had the opportunity to exercise his supposed larcenous streak. Even before he'd seen the last of Acton County Grammar School he was in a band, in fact The Who's prototype, The Detours. Early on it included the services of John Alex Entwistle, who in turn suggested they let a skinny bloke with a prominent honker who could play a bit of guitar join the group.

Enter Peter Townshend. The Detours at the time had evolved from its original inclinations towards skiffle, à la Lonnie Donegan, to early '60s pop, à la The Shadows. Roger was boss, the lead guitarist as well as the singer — he'd turfed out the original singer, Colin Dawson — and the drummer was Doug Sanden, years and years older than the others.

Entwistle was the trained one. His parents had separated just after he was born (October 9, 1946) and he lived with his grandparents more often than not. Growing up alone, he withdrew into his own imagination drawing great *Boris The Spider* like images and fiddling around on the piano. He had talent and was given music lessons. He went on to play French horn, joined the Middlesex Youth Orchestra, but finally strayed from the straight and narrow and ended up in a little combo that played ersatz Dixieland. Pete Townshend played banjo, Entwistle played trumpet, and they had the unlikely name (for a trad band, anyhow) of The Scorpions.

Roger thinks The Detours may have been the first band around London at the time to go from pop to hardcore rhythm'n'blues — hardcore R'n'B as they eventually billed themselves. One thing's sure, something kicked over their ignition and they went from idle to overdrive. And that something was Keith Moon.

NEW YORK

Early pictures of Moonie show a sad-eyed little kid with a smile that curved down from under a fixed upper lip. The maximum imp. The last picture of him, the one paraded by newspapers after his death, shows much the same smile. He'd been sitting with his girlfriend, Annette Walter Lax, at the same table as a bearded David Frost at a party thrown by Paul McCartney to celebrate Buddy Holly's birthday, and the photographers had caught him as energized as ever. His face is chubbier but the little-kid-on-a-tear look is still there.

He'd wanted desperately to join The Detours. He was in The Beachcombers, a

TORONTO

CHICAGO

TORONTO

TORONTO

TORONTO

WASHINGTON, D.C.

BUFFALO

pseudo-Beach Boys band at the time, and although he never completely left behind a fondness for Beach Boys harmony, it wasn't much of a gig for a drummer. And it was no gig at all for the kind of drummer Keith Moon was.

"Looney" is one word the others have used with affection. The band, calling itself The Who by now, was looking for a drummer and Moon turned up ("...in ginger hair and a ginger suit with a ginger shirt," Daltrey remembers. "It was great."). He'd had a drink or two to screw up his courage and by the time his audition was finished he'd destroyed the drum kit. This impressed the others no end. It was their conviction that their lives were bringing them closer to the edge and here was someone sliding happily along it.

Musicologists can be brought in to determine when The Stones went from being a white rhythm'n'blues band to a rock band, or that precise moment The Beatles' own style took over from what they were borrowing. But The Who had the chance to become The Who the moment Keith Moon snapped off the bass drum pedal at the pub that day. All it needed was Pete Townshend to get them there.

Soon after Moon arrived, the power center within the group began to shift. Moon approached drumming as an outsider. He'd place accents where they weren't supposed to be, and his attack wouldn't coincide with what was expected. In truth, he had a problem with keeping time. It was as if he'd decided to play X's-and-O's by putting his X's on the grid work, and not in the squares where they were supposed to be. He saw it all from a different angle. His fills weren't fills at all, but side comments on what had gone before. Watching him work you'd swear he could be sitting back there, propped high above the stage, and *the band wasn't necessary.* He was liberating. This was exactly what Townshend was looking for.

Daltrey observes about the beginning: "When we first started playing, we talked about making records, but it was years after Pete joined before there were any signs of him taking over the writing completely. I've always admired his writing. But when he does his thing for himself it's not the same as when he writes for the band. Whatever he does on his own is not as strong as his writing for The Who.

"That was the magic of it all then, being there as Pete actually began to make his ideas work. We used to talk things over. But eventually we didn't even have to and Pete and I didn't have to say anything. We'd just communicate and it'd be very intense and we'd get the ideas across. It's funny now these days but we don't feel comfortable around each other. Not at all. We couldn't sit in a room opposite each other without anything to do. And after twenty years..."

He smiles, brilliantly: "I did love the man, though. Don't let anyone ever come between us because I did love the man dearly. It was never the normal kind of relationship people could identify with and now that it's over, that's what hurts so much.

"Pete was the thing that made it happen for us. The first day he joined there was a difference. The whole thing of genius is that it's close to madness and it's the same with Pete. He is a schizophrenic character. He's got this side of him that loves the family and peace and love and all that. There's this other side of him that will shit all over you. Genius and madness. Pete sometimes slips from one to the other.

"I don't think I'm like that. No, not at all. I can live with myself quite easily. I like being alone. And I'm pretty happy. That's not to say that I don't get lonely. But I'm not an agonizing person like Pete.

"But we *all* have felt that we've had something important to do. We've never ever thought of quitting, not after Cincinnati, never. And I have the feeling that we're only beginning to get to it. It'll still come from Pete but it will be the band that does it.

"Maybe this is just me. I don't know. It's always been in me, this thing that's driving me on, because I've always known that *Tommy* wasn't the end of it for us.

"That's what *not* touring really could mean for us. I'm actually looking forward to the period when we're not signed up to anybody or to do anything. I'm fed up with all the crap that surrounds us. The business part of it is too big now. And I don't want to be part of any of it. I just want to make music. Being on the road puts limitations on a band. It makes you do what you don't really want to do.

PHILADELPHIA

"I'm not suggesting anything special. Right from the start The Who's been consistent in only one way — we're consistently inconsistent. Right from the start we've been four guys who like playing together. There has never been any greater drive to it than that. We've always had different opinions as to what kind of band we should be. John would like us to be a heavy metal band while I think The Who is an alternative to that kind of thing.

"Without having to go on the road we have so many more options. We can experiment more, come up with a lot of ideas and throw

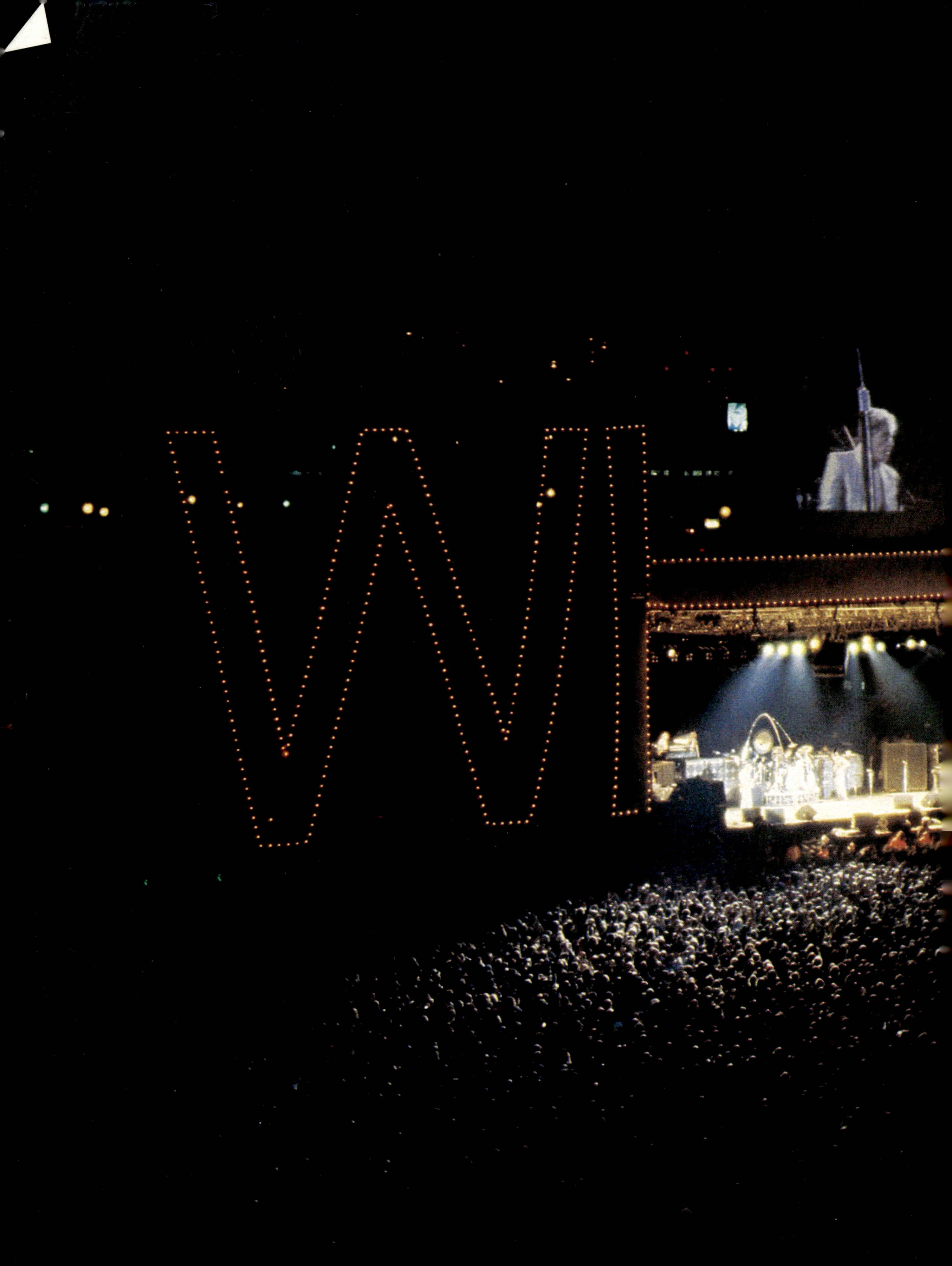

WASHINGTON, D.C.

PREVIOUS SPREAD
NEW YORK

'em against the wall to see what sticks. We can make an album with a 200-piece orchestra or vacuum cleaners. We could even do shows this way. We just wouldn't have to tour with them.

"That's exactly what I meant about the restrictions imposed by touring. At least we've stopped while we're on top rather than see us go downhill. And that certainly was in the cards for a band like The Who. We'd all be in our forties. Being in The Who does wear down your energy levels and I don't think we'd be quite the same band if we just went on and on. We're the kind of band that has to bring things to a finish.

"Getting older in itself doesn't bother me. I just find it hard to identify with being a rock'n'roll singer. My son is eighteen years old now. It seems like he should be the singer, not me.

"Besides, I want to do a lot of other things with my life. The one thing I hate about rock'n'roll is that process of album, tour, album, tour. It's rather bloody boring to be honest with you, and there are a lot of other things I want to do with my life that don't have to do with all that. Rock'n'roll has given me a lot but I've given a lot back and I just want to do other things.

"That doesn't mean an end to The Who. As long as Pete and John and I are involved together in something there'll be The Who. It's as simple as that. I don't include Kenney because in that area I don't think he's really a part. I think we'll make more films as The Who.

"And we'll change. A while back, when Pete was going through his problems, he stopped talking about our generation and was trying to speak for a younger generation which is a dangerous game. It seems strange that rock'n'roll has to be preoccupied with the pressures of adolescence. I think the pressures of middle age are worse. And I think Pete has done some good writing in that area. When he was engrossed with adolescence back then, it wasn't our generation he was writing about.

"What we've always been about is letting people's frustrations out. We always have done it. That's the secret of the success of The Who. We had this knack of writing what everyone was feeling and we could communicate. That's what we've always really done well."

The records themselves bring this out: *I'm The Face*, which they recorded in 1964 when they were still called the High Numbers, held up a mirror to the Mods. *My Generation* was the '60s first all-embracing battle cry. *The Who Sell Out* pricked the ballooning self-importance of the later '60s; *Who's Next* was even more critical of what they themselves had come to stand for.

CHICAGO

Chapter 5

The baby-boom Mods and rockers — or the North American equivalent of the same — have lots of unfinished business and The Who themselves are proof of that. Indeed, they've even been forcing the issue, with Townshend undercutting the notion that rock can go on forever, that it has no age limit. ("Absolute nonsense," he says succinctly.)

As long as they're out and about and as long as Townshend himself wants to keep talking about it, what his generation started isn't finished yet.

But we're getting ahead of ourselves here.

By mid-1964, The Who had acquired a manager. Pete Meaden had once worked for Andrew Loog Oldham of The Stones and he'd been hired by Helmut Gordon who wanted in on all the new excitement buzzing through London. Meaden's plan was simple — make The Who *the* Mod band. First he changed the name to The High Numbers, bridging two ideas, the Mod's idea of hipness and the hit parade's idea of success. He had them booked into the right Wardour Street club. And he got them on record, with *I'm The Face* (Slim Harpo's *Got Love If You Want It* revamped) backed with a piece called *Zoot Suit*. What he didn't do — at least what he hadn't anticipated — was The Who's live performances.

CHICAGO

NEW YORK

WASHINGTON, D.C.

They were chaotic. And unforgettable. They weren't just the band down the way, they were theater. They'd fight one another to grab attention. Moon was finding more and more ways to ignore the accepted rules and procedures of playing the drums. Townshend was experimenting with raw noise. Daltrey was finding his voice and how to use the stage. And they . . . started . . . breaking . . . things.

Pete's guitars. Moonie's drums. They'd get angry or frustrated or merely caught up in the on-rushing energy and whack! wham! fifty pounds of equipment would be flying across the stage.

But out of all this two distinct factors began to emerge. One was a mini-corporation called The Who, the other was Pete Townshend. Meaden was succeeded by Kit Lambert and Chris Stamp, two bright young men around town who were both as much interested in film as much as in rock but who still wanted to shape The Who. The other factor was Peter Townshend. No one shaped Pete Townshend.

WASHINGTON, D.C.

Lambert and Stamp wanted them to change the name (after all, "High Numbers" actually meant something, Top of the Pops and all that; "The Who" was an absolutely confusing title in just about any context imaginable. It was, therefore, perfect.). Pete Townshend, art school ideas floating around his head, took the intelligent amateur's approach to rock and started ignoring its rules while changing it radically.

Lambert and Stamp urged them to fix their capital-L Look — the hair, just so, the clothes, nouveau. Townshend thought raw noise was interesting. Lambert and Stamp arranged their appearances in local pubs. Townshend was cranking the dials on his amps up to 10 — loud had never been quite so LOUD before. Lambert and Stamp were getting recording contracts. Townshend was writing *My Generation*.

PHILADELPHIA

This song of course could also be called the first great scam of the '60s when it came out. I mean, for everyone who actually *believed* the words, there was someone who was devastated by the performance. The words? Well, I understood the part about people who "put us d-d-down." Anyone without a crewcut back in 1966 knew what that meant. However, I was never completely in sympathy with, as Pete said, "my commitment to 'Hope I die before I get old' which I've had great difficulty living with." (Old is purely relative, right?) But when

PHILADELPHIA

LOUISVILLE

Daltrey started stuttering "f-f-f-f" well, damn, he began driving radio programmers and nice folks up the wall. (One reason given why the stutter — they recorded it in a cold studio that day.) It was great. Consciously or not, The Who had found society's soft spot, the only place a middle-class revolution might be successful. It wasn't anything as formal as a class or generational conflict. It was through the mere *possibility* of naughty words. "Fade away," indeed.

But here's where the first of The Who's troubles began. The Beatles and The Stones — not to forget Herman's Hermits — appeared to North America much as they had back home in England. Not The Who. While Manchester kids were hearing *I Can't Explain*, the band's first single as The Who in 1965, North American kids first heard *Happy Jack* in 1966. *Happy Jack*, with its clipped, stop-start rhythm, only made the band seem slightly quirky, not powerful.

A following tour with the aforementioned Herman's Hermits didn't help matters much. The power of The Who's first live shows — the very first one in North America came in Brooklyn in 1967 — was only discovered by those who'd seen them. It took word coming back from the crowd who'd been at the Monterey Pop Festival and finally seen the film itself to focus the image of the band's sheer, intense power.

And The Who's power is unlike anything else in rock. As with others of their generation, they'd learned from black music and began by playing it: people at the very earliest gigs remember their rhythm'n'blues cover versions. Unlike many of the other bands of their generation — The Stones, for instance — The

YAMAHA
HIWATT

CHICAGO

CHICAGO

PREVIOUS PAGE
CHICAGO

CHICAGO

Who had an entire musical style between what they began doing and where their music had come from.

You can still hear some Chuck Berry in what Keith Richards does. Townshend's playing goes one step further. To put it — or hear it — another way: something black will always be in The Stones' music: The Who are one of the whitest bands ever to play rock'n'roll.

Moon brought the band its increasing share of notoriety because of his various boozed-out binges which destroyed a number of hotel

PHILADELPHIA

LOUISVILLE

rooms and a corresponding number of television sets in those hotel rooms.

Moon's madness overshadowed a change in Townshend which would in turn radically alter what the band was all about — and how it would be seen. His studies with Meher Baba, the Indian guru, led him to *Tommy* and the rock opera, so called, about "the deaf, dumb and blind boy." The music itself — particularly *Pinball Wizard* and *I'm Free* — brought the band to an even larger audience throughout 1969 and 1970. The movie version which appeared was the deciding factor in taking them to that still larger audience that went beyond rock.

OAKLAND

OAKLAND

Perhaps its first two albums of the '70s, *Live At Leeds* and *Who's Next*, represent the band at its peak. Never had they sounded better (*Live At Leeds* is positively ethereal). Never did their music sound so *sure* (as in *Baba O'Riley*). But things started to come loose when the band was jolted by a series of shocks, first Moon's death in 1978 and, a year later, the death of eleven fans before a Who concert at Cincinnati's Riverfront Coliseum.

"Keith — he'd been unhappy for some time," Roger told me, as he was staring off into a corner in his room. "Before his death we'd had several narrow escapes, when he'd OD on something and we'd have to walk him around the room. We had to cancel a few shows because of this. He felt guilty about losing his first wife, I think. Incredibly guilty. He loved her very very much but it was a really love-hate thing. That's what did it."

They had married in 1966, Keith and Kim Kerrigan. She was just sixteen, blond and pretty — "every woman he went out with after looked like her," Roger remembers —

OAKLAND

and to Kit Lambert she was nothing but trouble. She was robbing the band of one of its sex symbols. The real troubles were of a different kind. Living with Keith was not easy to say the least, what with everyone dropping in all the time at their flat. Then she kept hearing about his antics on the road — smashing TV sets because of room service foul-ups, hacking his way through walls, dressing up in drag, crashing a Lincoln into a swimming pool. Kim left him several times, worried about the effect all this craziness was having on their daughter, Mandy. Finally she couldn't take it any longer. She left for good in 1974.

Roger: "He used to love her so intensely. But he'd fight with her all the time — he couldn't live without her, you know. And I think he never forgave himself for that — having let her go. But who knows? Once we had to cancel a couple of shows at Madison Square Garden because he'd OD'd on something and a couple of days later I went to see him.

LOUISVILLE

CHICAGO

"I thought I'd figured out the key to his problems, losing his wife and kid, and I told him he was killing himself over it. He owned up and said, yes, that was it. But I don't know if he was telling the truth or not. At other times, we'd talk about it again and he'd burst into tears and say, 'ya, that's it.'

"Still, half the time he was married he didn't see her. And after they were apart he wouldn't go and visit her. He changed a bit eventually. But he never forgave himself until it was too late. He was quite violent. He'd punish himself for losing her. She was a much bigger thing in his life than anyone thought.

"We're normal people in so many ways, The Who I mean. But things keep happening. I don't know. After Cincinnati we had so many people stick by us. So many bands shit on their fans; they don't talk to the kids or anything. But we've never done that. The Who really does care for its fans."

WASHINGTON, D.C.

Too many interests outside their relation with their fans took its toll through the '70s, he feels. He was acting. John had his own band for his own songs — pieces that never seemed to fit into what The Who were doing. And for Townshend there was his *own* new music. They produced *Quadrophenia* in 1973, but Pete came to think of it as his first solo album in its way. He also recorded *Rough Mix* with Ronnie Laine.

But it was a crisis waiting to happen and Moon's death brought it to a head. Without him, The Who weren't exactly The Who anymore, something Daltrey believes to this day. And he's not alone in this feeling. Audiences missed Moon — in fact, Kenney Jones, Moon's replacement, has said he has only started feeling comfortable with this current tour.

The group's career took on a self-seeking nature: two movies, "Quadrophenia" and "The Kids Are All Right," showed its deepening obsession with its own history. And Townshend, recording more and more on his own,

WASHINGTON, D.C.

had become more and more introspective. The Who weren't about to break up. They were imploding.

And it was Townshend's own self-destruct which was triggering it. Call it the mid-life crisis come early. He'd left his wife Karen — he'd met Karen Astley in art school — and their kids Emma and Minta, but he was anything but the new bachelor on the loose. He was deeply troubled, as Daltrey points out: "He was reacting to something, I don't know exactly what. But it wasn't just me. He was looking for something much bigger than my reaction."

He'd fly from London to Paris or New York or Los Angeles on pleasure trips. But mostly he hung around the bright new clubs around London and the bright new people there. And he drank more and more brandy, took more and more pills and cocaine. He was busy writing songs and was working on a book of short stories, too. But he was mostly busy escaping until one night, after one remarkable bout of excess, he had to be rushed to hospital. He nearly died. His mates knew Pete needed something to snap him out of it — they had to take The Who off his back, and break it up totally, or they had to make it matter to him again.

They did both.

"The Who was in a very fragile state for three years with us fighting to get Pete back on the road," Roger goes on. "He didn't want to do it — until his death he said he didn't want to do it. Nobody really knew he was in a bad way until near the end. He'd go and see his kids and that upset him. He knew he had to use his craft to get back but he couldn't. It would have been a nightmare for us, knowing he was in such a bad state, if we couldn't have done something for him. Talking him into touring gave him something to fight for."

Ironically, The Who's farewell gave them an extra jolt of life — and a brand-new audience, fans who were infants when The Who had already started recording. But the new generation recognizes something in this band it doesn't see in others, even those closer to its own age. It has to do with The Who's understanding of the audience itself; of what it feels like to be lumped in with everyone else your age. The band's original audience may have forgotten this. Its current crowd certainly hasn't — this gut understanding of what "generation" actually means. "I personally haven't enjoyed the last two years with Pete being in a bad state and falling apart," Daltrey goes on. "I've been very miserable. Worse, all of it was getting sad and pathetic and that really made me angry.

"You see, I can take anything from Pete. I can take him being a bastard. I can take him being a genius. I can't take him being pathetic. He was really pathetic in the last two years and it really destroyed me. I really must be getting conservative. But to see a guy you admire so much going off the rails taught me not to do the same thing. He preached all about bloody love and peace yet he stayed away from it.

"Worse, I had the feeling that he wasn't totally out of control. I think he knew what he was doing. I think he knew exactly what my reactions were. He was in total control. I don't think it had a lot to do with the band, either. I think the band itself was falling apart with problems. Peter can't live with mediocrity any more than I can, and with the band becoming mediocre, that got to him.

NEW YORK

"It cramped his style. He could be brilliant on his own, and I mean really brilliant. But he couldn't do that if he had to keep writing for The Who, too. To be totally good on your own is a selfish thing and you can't be selfish in a band. I think we might have stopped after Keith died. I regret we went on after we learned Pete had signed a contract for a solo career. That way, we would have freed him to do his solo career. I think he would have gotten bored and started up The Who again.

"This way The Who could do something without diversions. I listened to his solo albums which I like very much and there are songs on each of them that would have been good for The Who. Listening to them I kept thinking, 'That was a brilliant album The Who missed.' So he ended up having his first album being stronger than the second and with everything being watered down. I know it's the group that's being selfish. It's the group demanding too much from Pete. But he's the writer. It can't be any other way. It would have been a much easier way out if the group had ceased to exist when Keith died.

"We didn't really discuss breaking up at the time. We talked about it a bit when we had to re-sign our record contract. I remember I looked Pete in the eye and said, 'Can you come up with material because you know it's going to have to be you. I can't write songs.'

"I looked at him across the room and the deal was signed. Maybe one day I'll be able to write songs. But I try and try and nothing comes out. He's a genius at it. I can pilfer his stuff, but I can't do it on my own.

"When Moonie died, and when we knew Pete had signed on to do a solo career, it was the time we might have quit, too. This time, the effect of ending it all should be good, I think. I'll be getting more into acting. Pete will be making music, John too. We'll go on."

FOLLOWING PAGE
CHICAGO

TORONTO

Chapter 6

In April, 1982, Michael Cohl knew something that might be to his advantage.

Cohl is bearded and soft-spoken. He promotes rock shows, generally in Toronto, Canada, and like many others in this line of business he knew long before the press or public did that The Who were about to give the longest farewell since Napoleon trudged back from Russia.

That wasn't where he had his edge, though. This came from knowing what Bill Curbishley was thinking about — video.

Curbishley is the

WASHINGTON, D.C.

LOUISVILLE

band's manager, the only other vote in major decisons, and he'd worked with Cohl for years with each Who tour. As they talked, they began plotting the tour's finale even before it had begun — video. Cable TV. Pay TV. A spectacle.

And before Roger Daltrey was telling a press conference in New York that the band would give farewell tours "in every country where we've been successful," Cohl was already working out a way that the last gig in North America would come from his city in his building, Maple Leaf Gardens, and under his own conditions.

But there was competition. Various cities were being considered, with Cleveland being a front runner. Cleveland was solid Who country, an industrial town hard hit by the recession and traditionally given to liking the loudest, toughest rock bands coming down the pike. Better, it shared much of the same market as Detroit, and Detroit was where The Who had its first hit in North America with *My Generation.*

But Cohl figured he had an advantage. The cable-cast, no matter where it originated, would reach, in the States, most of the same cities the band had already played in. But if it came from a Canadian city, it could hit Canadian markets that the band had passed by. Admittedly, the Canadian market wouldn't equal what The Who could reach in California alone, but a potential audience of six or seven million was still a potential audience of six or seven million, a fact that is difficult for a promoter to ignore.

En route to the deal, at press conferences in Los Angeles Pete said that he liked Toronto because although it was North American to the last sheet of glass on its latest office tower, "there was something unique, maybe European about it."

CHICAGO

LOUISVILLE

OAKLAND

TORONTO

Cohl is a little less romantic about it. He could give the band a tax advantage and a market it should try to reach. The band bought the package.

But as with everything connected with The Who, it was not too wrapped up *that* smoothly and the Canadian segment of the telecast almost fell through. First of all, no Canadian network wanted the concert. Cohl was stunned. Here was Schlitz willing to shell out a seven-figure sum just to be associated with The Who, and Canadian TV was ducking it. Eventually, one — the CTV network — did come on board but was forced out of the game at the last moment by the American cable network which didn't want all those *free* Canadian television signals crossing the nearby border into U.S. cities where Pay TV was selling the telecast at anywhere from $10 to $12 a show. With CTV gone, Cohl had to scramble and an informal network across the country was set up at the last moment.

Ironically, the tour itself did go smoothly. For a while there, after the Cincinnati disaster, a brief stab was made at making The Who rock's bad boys. Author John G. Fuller analyzed the Cincinnati tragedy in his book, *Are The Kids Alright?*, and came up with the idea that, no, the kids were not alright. "The Rock Generation And Its Hidden Death Wish," was the subtitle.

But that wasn't the way things were to work out. As close as the kids would come to not being alright came at New York's Shea Stadium concerts in mid-October where various minor injuries were sustained in the crush of people coming to the show. Altogether, the smooth-as-silk Stones' cross-country tour of '81 seemed to set a pattern for The Who to follow.

"You'll notice how the tour mirrored what The Stones did before, playing Philadelphia about the same time they did, and so on down the line?" said one promoter along the way. He wasn't being cynical. "They're being practical this time out. This is future money they're making."

It was forty cities, half a million fans and a $23-million gross for the first half of the tour which ended in Tempe, Arizona, October 31. Accounting is still going on, and may always be, but the $23 million figure escalated to $40 million at the tour's end. The concerts kept getting better and the band kept getting more and more tired as the December 17th final concert in Toronto loomed larger and larger.

Roger eventually was so exhausted the press people with him on the road couldn't talk him into doing a six-minute bit backstage for ABC's "Good Morning America" — even though it would be a perfect plug for the final pay TV show. At the beginning, they were on the "Today Show" on NBC and CBS's "PM Magazine." But enough was enough.

Not knowing this, another PR firm, this one in Toronto, set up yet one more press conference, this one for 1 P.M. the afternoon The Who were to arrive in town. This too fell through, mainly because Toronto Airport was fogged in and the band had to drive across the border from Buffalo. Still, the PR-man's chutzpah was marvelled at. "Is he kidding?" said yet another public relations specialist. "These guys don't even know there is a one in the afternoon."

Eventually, another press conference time was set up and there the band sat, answering questions they'd answered earlier on the tour — questions lobbed their way by reporters who'd *asked* them earlier on the tour.

Actually, Townshend again did most of the talking; the others looked as if they'd already retired. Standing at the back of the room, a young woman caught Kenney's eye and winked. He smiled slightly. Why is the last tour ending in Toronto?"Because it's special,"Townshend explained.

Cohl's people had their own answer for that. They thought it was because of "small" gestures like sending a sushi chef over to the visiting team's dugout to cook for the band during its CNE Grandstand concert in October. For Supertramp, they'd sent over a monogrammed table-tennis table.

Reviews were good for the most part, although not everyone was charmed. Paul Sullivan of the *Chicago Tribune* called them "a band that refuses to learn a lesson."

He went further in a syndicated piece: "One of the greatest rock'n'roll bands of all time has suddenly become one of the most

TORONTO

NEW YORK

PREVIOUS SPREAD
LOUISVILLE

hypocritical bands of all time."

His complaint? The Who's tour should not be sponsored by Schlitz beer considering alcohol has been the source of much of its "tragedy-marred" past. He points to drummer Keith Moon's death, four years ago, through an overdose "on a drug he was taking to combat his alcoholism"; the death of eleven fans before a Who concert in Cincinnati three years ago after someone "tossed a whiskey bottle through a glass entrance door" at Riverfront Coliseum; and then there's Townshend himself who "revealed in an interview why he has become a reformed alcoholic."

Townshend told a press conference in Los Angeles that the main reason The Clash opened most of their open-air shows was because they were "my favorite band." This view reportedly was *not* shared by everyone backstage. In fact, there was a clash at one point between The Clash's people and The Who's.

Bruce Springsteen turned up at a party after the band's concert in Phoenix, Arizona, at the end of the tour's first leg. He talked to Daltrey privately for almost an hour; in fact, he was missed by almost everyone else in the room until a photographer taking photos for a trade magazine had "one more shot left" so he suggested Roger pose with that guy he was with.

The Boss showed up at the first concert in Springfield, Ohio, just south of Cleveland. "I've always loved them from the time I was sixteen playing *My Generation*," he said.

The Who's tour crisscrossed with dozens of others, many of them bands whose members are younger than The Who's own kids. Martin Fry of the band ABC, flush with his first discovery of success in America, nevertheless said he "couldn't even begin to think about what The Who are doing — I mean who can think that far ahead?" Others I talked to were equally mystified about what it meant. It was as if that band they listened to on record, the one they still had to compete with in the marketplace, and the one out there on the road, guys approaching their late 30s, were two different things; as if The Who as product was one thing, but The Who as part of the process was entirely different. "I always thought there'd always be The Who, like there'd always be Beatles' songs or Mick Jagger," said one young guitarist. "They weren't a band to me the way The Clash is a band. This is hard to explain, but it doesn't matter to me if The Who quit or not. They're already a part of history."

The implications of The Who's quitting were considerably more immediate to those who were caught in much the same trap, though. For all those out there with careers-in-progress — the radio programmers, magazine publishers, studio owners — who can coolly regard rock as a business, there are those — the deejays, the interviewers and the musicians themselves who must treat it in some way as their life. What seemed such a luxury at one time, living your work, had now become a burden. How do you quit *your life?* I mean, Ricky Nelson, whose music I like more than I can understand, once told Merv Griffin he had a breakdown just worrying about things like

OAKLAND

this. This is Ozzie and Harriet's kid for heaven's sakes.

I happened to cross paths one day with Klaus Voorman, one time intimate of The Beatles and now a producer of Trio, a trio of German minimalists. He understood exactly what The Who were going through. "You can't live up to the public's expectations," he was saying one day. "You can't let someone else's nostalgia get in the way. There are a lot of people who are hanging on but who should let go like The Who. Elton John for instance. He had to give up so much of himself to make it and now he can't let it go. I like him and I understand his feelings. It's difficult to get out of this life."

The new bands were out there, arriving in cities just behind or ahead of The Who and in some cases — Joe Jackson opening an October show in Toronto — coming with them. No one mistook The Who for the new thing certainly. Nor were they lumped in with the old. *It's Hard* even received a grudgingly complimentary review in *Trouser Press*. Yet you could sense that American radio's resistance to the new music coming from Europe had worn thin and, for some, playing Who music as the band came through town, was the first step to programming performers a generation younger.

Daltrey was thinking about this at one point during the tour: "New people keep coming

NEW YORK

NEW YORK

through. We came through in our generation and other groups now are coming through for this one. With all the stuff that's out there right now, there might be ten new groups a week going into the Top 20 in England. Only a few of them will stick, I realize. I don't know if The Human League will make it. I think their album is brilliant and their single classic pop. And The Clash — they've been around for a long time. They've done it. They've stuck. But I think the more pop changes, the more people are getting up there and more instant everything is, the better it is for everyone.

"It's dreadful when groups like us continue to dominate. That's why I like England and the English scene. We sell out shows and a lot of people hate us because we are so successful. I love that."

Come…

At a stopover in Orlando, Florida, the band runs into women's field hockey tournament. Knowing a bit of potential pure craziness

NEW YORK

LOUISVILLE

when it's at hand, The Who challenged one of the teams to a match.

But that's not all. To get fully into the spirit of it all, the band bought some green women's field hockey uniforms, complete with numbers, and played the game in these. It worked. The score ended up a 1-to-1 tie.

And join the party...

As the tour begins, John Entwistle begins to feel rather subconscious about his greying hair. He tints it. By the end, I was told, he only felt self-conscious because it was thinning.

LOUISVILLE

TORONTO

Chapter 7

The moment I meet Townshend I remember how amazing his eyes are, those spacy blues. Seeing him in repose always comes as a surprise. I mean, he's not mid-way through some manic leap. What isn't a surprise is listening to him. You realize immediately you *know* that voice, if not its sound at least the sense of it.

We grew up with rock'n'roll and grew up with it in many different ways. One way, I realized on this tour, was something of a secret. We heard the stuff and some of us lived the life; some managed, others promoted, hustled, sold, bought and borrowed it.

But we also *read* about it right from the start. That was the secret, one we kept from ourselves by not recognizing its importance. And almost from the start we could read what was said by its most articulate critic — Pete Townshend. As quickly as anyone could come to know a particular sound — Janis Joplin's voice or David Bowie's, say — you came to recognize a Townshend quote.

NEW YORK

OAKLAND

NEW YORK

NEW YORK

It was part of rock's early lore and if rock writing had a star subject, he was it. And as you came to cherish certain songs or albums, you came to retain things he'd said — like about his nose. His decision to become a great and world famous rock star, he'd said, was due to the fact that kids at school — he was born into a musical family in Chiswick, May 19, 1945 and attended Acton County Grammar School — kidded him about his nose. As revenge he decided to become so well known that he'd "push this huge hooter at them from every newspaper in England."

Then there was the line about working with Daltrey: "If you don't go along his way you got his fist." Another famous quote comes from the beginning of the 1978 tour, when he was telling writers, "I've burned myself out." He in fact had explained to *Rolling Stone* magazine the entire substance of *Tommy* before it had come out — "It's going to be extremely difficult — but we want to try to do it musically" — and explained to American hippies what British Mods were all about.

Ironically — for him anyhow — he'd been most silent about what was the most consequential period of his life — his two-year binge. A listen to any of the band's albums from the mid-'70s on, or to *Empty Glass* or *All The Best Cowboys Have Chinese Eyes*, might have revealed the search he was making and

NEW YORK

WASHINGTON, D.C.

the pain at not finding what he was after. But that wasn't the same. In the past, he would have explained it and himself over and over again.

On *The Who By Numbers* the introspection begins in earnest culminating in *I Am An Animal* from *Empty Glass.* On *Who Are You*, in 1978, the band's back in business even if his doubts cut through the bright well-crafted surface. By the time *Face Dances* was released two years later, the doubts had taken over. As had the booze.

Years ago he'd explained to writers what his generation and his band were about; that being a Mod was "the highest form of transcendence," and that being in The Who was an extension of that. It was an escape except that everyone had escaped with you. ("The baby boomers are their environment," writes Landon Jones in *Great Expectations: America and the Baby Boom Generation.* Townshend understood that instinctively right from the start.) But as any sense of unanimity crumbles, escape must be increasingly personal. For the band, getting out on the road was enough. "This is where you forget," he told Jann Wenner of *Rolling Stone.* "You don't want to take things seriously, you just let things pour out, and often they are the wrong things."

But what happens when the band, this Mod microcosm, begins to fall apart? Well, there's booze and pills and London's Wardour Street and the Venue and the "oblivion seekers" of the '80s.

The "oblivion seekers" is not my own phrase. It comes from a short story by Isabelle Eberhardt, a remarkable woman born in Geneva in 1877 who searched for spiritual wisdom and found it in Sufism. "The seekers of oblivion sing and clap their hands lazily; their dream voices ring out late into the night, in the dim light of the mica-paned lantern," she writes in a Paul Bowles' translation. "Such men can reach the magic horizon where they are free to build their dream-palaces of delight."

In 1968, Townshend came across Meher Baba, the religious leader who was anointed as a perfect master after a kiss by a Sufi saint and whose philosophy, such as it was, of tranquil joy appealed to him. Baba inspired him to look at the possibility of a larger project — he'd already begun a longer piece with the song

WASHINGTON, D.C.

NEW YORK

Rael from *The Who Sell Out* — which would eventually lead to *Tommy*. And here, too, the idea of oblivion fascinated him with the deaf, dumb and blind boy.

In *Empty Glass*, he looked at complete selfishness — and at responsibility. A kind of magic palace could be found with the New Romantics and the Club for Heroes where he dallied. And he could avoid responsibility through his many and varying addictions which included Ativan, ending only after the expert help of Meg Patterson, the California detoxification specialist. What he really wanted to find, he tells me in his hotel suite one day, was himself. One reason he stopped drinking was because he wanted to be a part of his own life: "If someone wants to shake my hand, I want him to be able to shake *my* hand and not the hand of somebody that he thinks he knows."

And he had to face his family — again. "My family knows about all the stuff that happened

NEW YORK

to me and I know at the moment I am feeling more loved and in more direct contact with my kids than I could ever expect to experience considering the kind of life that I live. I treasure the fact they do know me a bit better.

"My wife gets really upset about reading stuff in the papers about me that she is not familiar with or hasn't heard about before from me, or thinks is too private. But I feel you should be as honest as possible. I'm friendly with David Bowie and he has the opposite attitude. We went out to dinner with him and his girl friend and he told us what he did — that he had to keep everything to himself because they would use it against him because they'd screw him and because they'd manipulate him.

"But who's this 'they' I wondered? Does he actually believe there is this great conglomerate of journalists who have this telephone

CHICAGO

system? It's the people on the street who determine what appears about people in newspapers. If you tell the truth about yourself — tell it like it is — then even if it's edited and manipulated and even if only part of the truth gets out, at least it's *partly* true. If you sit there lying through your teeth or saying nothing, then people make stuff up.

"I remember when after the Cincinnati disaster our manager, rightly or wrongly, decided not to make a statement that evening. There was a load of card-carrying reporters who went back to the phones and made up statements. I know how they felt. They were waiting outside a fucking hotel for five hours trying to get a story on which their careers rested. They knew people wanted a story so they said what they thought we would say.

"So I told David Bowie I couldn't live with doing things that way. I couldn't keep myself completely private. That's the way he chooses to do it and when I want to talk to him on the telephone I have to go through forty secretaries to get through to him. He gives me his telephone number and tells me not to give it to anyone else. But when you phone him he's changed it."

Some coffee is poured and he lights another tiny, Indian cigarette: "I'll tell you one thing if you really want to be candid. The only thing I find difficulty with when I've not had a drink, is sex. I'm sort of shy. Socially, I don't give a fuck. I'm not anti-alcohol. I think it's a wonderful thing. And I think it does have its place in society. I think it has opened doors which would otherwise not be opened. There are books about alcoholism and writers. And there's the belief that the Hemingways and Scott Fitzgeralds of this world actually believed that they couldn't write sober, that their writing voice actually came from the condition they were in, rather than from inside themselves, so in fact they didn't actually understand what was happening.

"For me, I know that there are certain things I won't be able to do and certain things I won't be able to create without being drunk, but I wouldn't say that they were the most treasured aspects of what I've done. I mean,

WASHINGTON, D.C.

some of the things I've written that way have been the most dangerous things I've written.

"You know, the thing about being drunk is that you sober up. You might write a song when you are drunk but when you go to record it in a studio the day after you are sober. It's not what you thought it was. When you're drinking you might forget yourself or forget some of the things that you are bothered about. You might play better or a bit more loosely. But I think all that's possible *without* booze. I think the hands, the body and the subconscious remember things and are capable of things and booze isn't needed.

"Before we started to tour America a lot I used a lot of uppers. But I stopped using everything in 1967 and never used anything again until the last couple of years. For me, it was always the stimulants I was after. When I drank, I drank brandy because it stimulates you. I don't like the feeling of being clouded over too much. There's no substitute for adrenalin. Often what happens is you walk out onstage drunk and within two minutes you are stone cold sober. You do a show completely sober: it's as if adrenalin rises above it. But when you walk off, you're drunk again."

Well, I tell him, what has always struck me is the constant high level of energy they've always been able to maintain: "That," he said, "is an indication of drugs, alcohol and artificial stimulants.

"You know, it's really weird, but there have been whole tours which have taken place and I've been drunk from start to finish. But I can remember every second of every gig, because those were the little fragments where I got my body to work and the blood to flow. I was okay then."

The Who, he points out, has been most together onstage. Offstage it's always been another matter, what with Roger being booted out around the time of *My Generation* and years later, after Moon's death, Roger not wanting a new drummer and Pete wondering about adding another guitarist and everyone concerned about money.

"Hmm," says Townshend. "The Who has never been any one thing at any one time and all the changes came from how we were as individuals at any given time. There have been times when I've been drinking and there was a time over 1975-1976 I stopped drinking for eighteen months. There have been times we have been completely straight. There have been times when Keith was magnificently healthy and times when he was a drug addict — although either way, he was a magnificent player.

"I remember when we started a lot of people used to say, 'the only reason you're doing what you're doing — all that leaping about — is because you're on something.'

"Actually, it's never been all that difficult, all that leaping about. If all you had to do over two hours is shuffle your feet every now and again, move backwards and forwards between a microphone and an amplifier then do, say, ten drop kicks — well, I think in two hours you can manage that without getting a heart attack or working up much of a sweat. It's like watching 'Chariots of Fire' and all the running seems so much more dramatic because of Vangelis' music in the background.

"Anyway, when we started there was a tremendous shared ambition in the band to play everybody else in the rock business off the stage, however long it took. I felt it personally.

WASHINGTON, D.C.

FOLLOWING PAGE PHILADELPHIA

"I remember once saying to Eric Clapton just after Jimi Hendrix had first appeared on the scene and both of us were enamoured with him — I said, 'One day I'll play him off the stage.'

"He just said, 'Fuck off.'

"'No, I will,' I said.

"At that time I realized that I had to say that. I had to believe it, even though I felt there was no way I could. Although Jimi helped me out there. It was like being the champion by default. Part of The Who's philosophy, one of the things that's consistently driven us, has been this need to keep working, working, always working.

"We had to because we never knew what we'd come up with next. Just when we'd think we'd achieved everything we wanted to, we'd be surprised by something we'd do. I think The Who is stopping touring now, not because we're not capable of anything else, but because we want to look for surprises elsewhere.

"There was never any kind of idea behind

OAKLAND

NEW YORK

the band. There has been image consciousness. I was conscious of the image of the group, coming from art college and wanting the band to look a particular way, knowing the value of fashion, knowing that an artist is more important than his art.

"To start with, nobody would listen to what we had to say unless we looked right and acted right. We had to be to some extent larger than life and I knew as individuals we didn't have natural charisma. It had to be added. I tend to be obsessive about that. Roger for his part was obsessed with making the band act like a unit. The word he used all the time was 'drive.'

"There were certain ideas we started then and kept up and which are still very much with us today; certain principles that we've stuck to. The other factor which affected us early on was living in the shadow of The Beatles who were such great innovators. The Beatles did so many things first that it sent you to sleep listening to the list of them. The most important thing that they did was first to introduce innovation, chance and danger.

"About the Beatles — they were a pop phenomenon, and if you view their work, just as it was, without all the kerfuffle around it, their music is not always very vital. It's a lot like classical music. A lot of it is like the kind of stuff that you could imagine an Italian composer working for RCA would produce for Sophia Loren to sing. I felt they were producing really reactionary derivative material for a long time.

"But they were there. Up above everyone else. They were even bigger than Herman's Hermits. Hah. Like Elvis, they were completely inaccessible. When The Beatles became physically accessible is when I started to feel really emotionally involved in their work. I think my view changed a little bit and I felt less antagonistic toward them.

"I suppose I have always categorized them differently than The Stones. I would even say The Kinks were a better rock band than the Beatles. That's just *my* definition of rock and I've come to regret a *Rolling Stone* interview I did because I found myself starting to categorize music again and that's bad. When you try to define rock by definition you categorize it.

CHICAGO

CHICAGO

"I mean, one of the things often said about rock is that it's great because it embraces everything. That's fine, but you know there's a lot it embraces that is of no interest to me, a lot I feel is unimportant. I suppose I've always taken my music fairly seriously and so I prefer The Beatles at their most serious and most academic.

"I still turn the radio off whenever I begin to hear *Michelle* and stuff like that come on. They have some masterpieces. *Yesterday* is the most recorded song in history but, to be quite honest, I feel that any good house writers could have written it.

"I appreciate any good music, it's very much a part of my life. I go and see new bands. I genuinely like the music because it's new and because it comes from young people — I am obsessed with adolescence to this day.

"But let me explain, and this may seem a little bit academic, but I am obsessed with things that happen to people. People are formed by everything around them and this works in rock, too. The same things happen to different generations; everybody goes through the same things. I hear a record on the charts by Human League or something and think, 'The Who have been making records like that for fifteen years.' People in new bands are now strutting around America saying, 'This is it. This is the beginning of the new British invasion. You can say goodbye to your old super groups of rock'n'roll because we're going to hit them where it hurts.'

"I don't panic because I've seen the Human League live. I don't panic because I've met the people and know the situation in which they work; I know the records and play them and like them and understand exactly what is happening on them. And I know how big America is and I know as well how you have to conquer it. I know how quickly you can disappear, too. I mean, there's a guy I used to help produce — Arthur Brown — who had a No. 1 single and a No. 1 album and that was it. After that, he was gone. Never seen again. So because that does happen, I don't react instantly when someone comes along making claims about the new this or that or the end of this or that.

WASHINGTON, D.C.

"It would be wrong for The Who to suddenly start to produce electro-pop, despite the fact we introduced it to some extent although when we did I didn't use it in a particular dangerous manner. We shouldn't produce electro-pop, or the new music wouldn't have anything to bounce off of.

"There's an analogy here to Russia and classical ballet and classical music. For years that was the only kind of dance seen there, one kind of music. There's no Harlem theater, no rock. They're the losers. We, in the West,

OAKLAND

CHICAGO

are the winners because we've got what they've got — Tchaikovsky and Rimsky Korsakov — while in New York we've got some of the finest classically trained dancers in the world — while we *also* have modern music and incredible innovators and crazy people. So in rock right now there are various traditions at work and I think that's good.

"The Who have said right from the very beginning that the traditions and limitations of rock, the ones which you use for yourself, are what make it so vital. We — The Who — are very much affected by the new music around us right now. But you don't have to be blown over by it. The band is like a reed to some extent. We get blown backwards and forwards by everything new that comes along. We bend with the changes but when the latest big wind has blown over we're still there, straight as before.

"Whereas The Stones, because Mick is influenced by fashion to a degree, might be influenced this way or that. But one reason *Tattoo You* is such a successful album is because it was a return to a slightly more formal Stones' sound. I get sick of hearing *Start Me Up* on the radio where it's played every fifteen seconds, but it's a great record.

"I was in L.A. in January and I heard the new wave station there. They just play new wave: 'We don't play dinosaurs,' they say, 'we just play new wave.' Okay, so you hear Soft Cell followed by Human League followed by Duran Duran. The Cars are okay they let you know, but they don't play The Who or The Stones.

"And that's a pity because they're missing something. What I've found missing on FM radio in America now was the way it was when we first played there and you'd hear on radio Charlie Mingus followed by The Rolling Stones. Music was in juxtaposition on earlier FM radio and it was great. An aggressive new star in radio programming is needed to get new music on the radio over here.

"Whatever 'new' is there, we're still there too."

CHICAGO

Chapter 8

In my rented midget car, I'm clunking up the interstate and listening to its tiny radio blare out The Pretenders' Chrissie Hynde sing *My City Was Gone*. It's about Akron, a city thirty miles behind me and, despite her harsh, aggressive vocal, it could not be more . . . *right*-sounding as I rattle through the middle of Cleveland's suburbs.

It's after the first of The Who's two nights at the Richfield Coliseum halfway between the two cities, and it may have been their finest moment on the tour. But it's Hynde I'm

BUFFALO

TORONTO

listening to now —
and her sad song about going
back to a home which has disappeared
and the train station that was gone, the downtown too and the pretty countryside "paved down the middle."

This impression isn't universally held here, of course. Things are looking up, as a couple of young business studs had told me as we'd

WASHINGTON, D.C.

been sitting around the lounge bar of the Stouffer's Inn On The Square hotel: lots of boosterism here. A recent survey by the Growth Association indicates that people aren't as fearful of the inner city as they used to be. Pianist Rudolf Firkusny and Lynn Harrell, former principal cellist of the Cleveland Orchestra, had passed through the weekend before — "elegant and refined," they were, said one critic. And they'd held the Western Reserve Junior Service League Candlelight Ball at the Kirtland Country Club where one woman wore a replica of the dress Princess Di had worn when she'd first appeared in public with Prince Charles.

But this was a different Cleveland than The Who played to. Their Cleveland was the one in the Ohio Chrissie Hynde was singing about; the one reeling from the recession, with young guys trying to make monthly payments on their vans, and their old ladies who scraped up enough cash for the tickets, couples sitting in the freezing parking lot circling the Coliseum drinking Pabst and Bud and fiery sips of Meadwood 100 Proof Straight Bourbon Whiskey; a man named Gerry who was selling pot by the joint even if the joints had frozen; and another guy named Randle who was a Pete Townshend look-a-like — is there a city without them?

Inside, Miami Steve Van Zandt looked cautiously at the squad of Cleveland reporters there for what was, after all, one of the last shows The Who would ever give in America. He was opening the concert, but that's not what they were interested in.

What exactly, they wanted to know, was his link with The Who? Well, he said, he'd been the first in his school to have a Who single. The first. Hmm, the reporters said. His boss, *The Boss*, Bruce Springsteen, there too, explaining that *he'd* loved them since he was sixteen and playing *My Generation*.

But no sooner was Miami Steve out onstage than he began to think he might be in the right place only at the wrong time. At least that's how he felt about it later. "It's not the size of the crowd, or anything like that," he told me eventually. "But . . . well, you know, this was a Who crowd. It wasn't waiting for me exactly."

Looking around in the stands: a boy in a yellow Euclid school jacket; another one with T-shirt reading: "You never forget your first girl." A couple in matching $18 T-shirts — The Who: American Tour '82. They're in their mid-thirties, they tell me, and have been Who fans from the '60s. He was in politics then, he's not anymore. "Everything changed for me — us — I guess," he said. "But they haven't."

He meant the band. "To me, they've stayed exactly the same and that's really important to me. It's as if they haven't gotten older or weaker or quieter or anything. It's not that I feel nostalgic about them. It's not that at all. They're just . . . the same."

Who are The Who? Townshend's right, of

course. Along the way most of his contemporaries have responded to fashion in one way or another. As they've changed, the meaning of what they do has changed as well. But not The Who, at least not *much*. They're that very first headlong dash into '60s rock continuing. Listen to them and I think you can hear the spirit behind the music.

How else could four Brits nearing middle age hit a crowd like this? Stadium rock has been formulated like FM radio but it's effect is something else again. It's like being inside a vast TV set. Watching the vast instant-playback screen flash commercials for the local FM station involved with the concert, or the one, "Schlitz Rocks America," I had the impression of watching the screen from the inside. Weird. This is beginning to get to me. How the hell can the band stand this night after night?

Needing a break, I head back up the stands through the crowd to a corner pub called Jacques' Lounge — "Public Welcome" — Beer $1.60, Jumbo Beer $3. On the TV, Danny White bullets a pass to Butch Johnson. Guys in AC/DC jackets and Grateful Dead T-shirts whooped as the Dallas Cowboys riddle the hapless Houston Oilers — the dreaded Cowboys, how long ago Every Rocker's perfect symbol of the rigor mortis of corporate America?

The inevitable roar from the hall brought the band on. As if we were still back in Washington, not Cleveland, Townshend bobbed out, whirled his arm, flayed down his hand and it was *My Generation*. Once again.

Now, though, the concert's behind me and Chrissie Hynde's song is through. As if it made a horrible mistake, the station immediately comes up with a series of mainstream rockers than leaves me numb. Why the hell is this stuff so bloody bad, I wonder, and I come near to putting the car off the road yanking the dial back and forth.

"Friends?"

From some little station comes the dry, white, raspy voice of a preacher.

"Friends?"

I stop dialing. Why not? I figure. I'll stay with it. It sounds like jazz.

WASHINGTON, D.C.

OAKLAND

OAKLAND

"Do you feel crushed by your . . . life? Can you see no way out of your . . . troubles? Well, let me tell you, friends, the Lord is there and the Lord knows, yes, he *does* know, absolutely; and he can see, deep, DEEP! into your heart and he understands the suffering and the unhappiness and all, ALL! that's unholy deep DEEP! inside you, and he knows . . ."

He's into one holy terror of a riff here and it's absolutely amazing. Nothing less. I've heard sermons like this before, in French and

Spanish as well as English, on car radio in Georgia and live in North Carolina and via shortwave in France; and when the preachers really wind it up it has reminded me of tape loops of the early musical avant-gardists — Steve Reich's *Come Out Tonight* was one piece I remember hearing — used to come up with, where the voice would loop and loop again through a sentence and eventually it became pure sound.

And this guy was on one of his loops, refining the words to their sound-sense, around and around, faster and faster and, of course! it was exactly what Townshend was getting into.

". . . and he knows everyTHING! . . ."

The Toronto video-cast was dutiful and well played, although not as many signed up for it as the U.S. cable system would have liked. But the music peaked in Cleveland right at the moment the band first walked on. Facing a crowd which, in the main, was closer to their

KLAND

OAKLAND

TORONTO

kids' ages than to their own, the band hit a pace that was accelerating all the way.

Later on we try to figure out why it worked live and so well on video. Later on, too, we try to come up with the answer to the very first question — "Who were The Who?" Why did this tour hit that old nerve and, as one kid I met said, "They've sold out." Mikal Gilmore's insightful piece in the *Los Angeles Herald Examiner* suggested "there was something in the spectacle of the event . . . that served to undermine [its] power . . . . Indeed, the guiding purpose of this tour seems not to be the defining of an audience so much as merely the possessing of one."

WASHINGTON, D.C.

There was something about this tour which went beyond the nostalgic ("it's the last time") or the cynical ("let's get the dough while we can"). Or just greed. (Dave Marsh, in *The Record*, notes: "At least with this extra million dollars The Who won't have to play together again because they're broke.") The "something" was romance — capital R romance. It was likely the last time a band will ever try to address itself to a generation. It'll likely be the last time a band of any stature would even *think* about the very idea, because rock's fractious now, with factions within factions.

I don't know about the others in that van leaving the Capitol Center, but I came to

TORONTO

understand why I had trouble understanding what The Who was all about. It was too obvious. They were Rock's *Last Romantics*.

That's the clue to The Who, if there is one. And it has to do with something Daltrey said at the beginning, this whole idea of belief in the band.

The Who is a process, not a package. As long as The Who were the process, that on-going process of making rock'n'roll, and as long as everyone believed in it, the kids were alright. But the fear was that they were being packaged, bound by business who didn't understand, and it was time to pack it in.

The TV cameras came looking for something they couldn't find and ended up with not everything that was there.

It was what Townshend was saying about Mods and his generation — the meaning came from being a part of it, not from what it would do.

WASHINGTON, D.C.

LOUISVILLE

TORONTO

NEW YORK

TORONTO

TORONTO

TORONTO

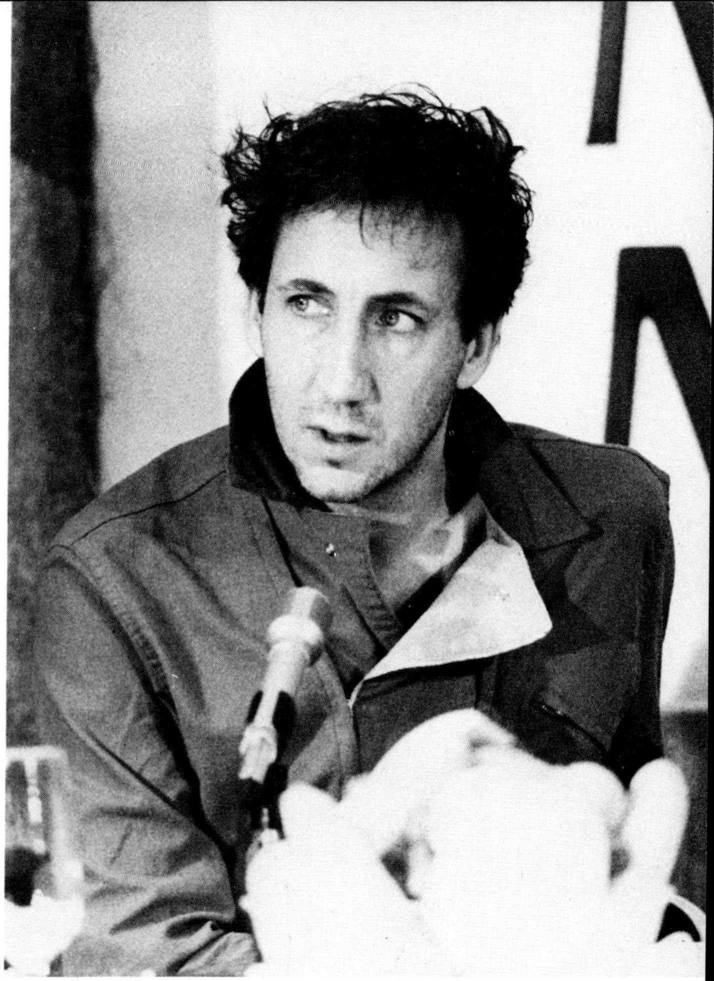

TORONTO

TORONTO

TORONTO

TORONTO

CHICAGO

CHICAGO

NEW YORK

TORONTO

TORONTO

FOLLOWING SPREAD
CHICAGO

MAHA

About the Authors

Photo by ALLAN STOKELL

Philip Kamin was born in Toronto on February 20, 1955, and makes this city his home. A graduate of Ryerson Polytechnical Institute, he picked up a camera for the first time in 1978 and went on the Genesis tour. His work met with instant success, and since then his photographs have appeared worldwide in magazines, songbooks, programs, publicity campaigns, and a book, and on album covers and posters. In addition to Genesis, Kamin has worked with: The Rolling Stones, The Who, Peter Gabriel, The Cars, Phil Collins, The Little River Band, Van Halen, Black Sabbath, Rod Stewart, Triumph, Ian Hunter, Teenage Head, Martha And The Muffins, Roxy Music, Ian Dury.

Kamin's first book, co-authored by Peter Goddard, is titled *The Rolling Stones Live* (in the U.S., *The Rolling Stones: The Last Tour).*

Philip Kamin uses Canon cameras and equipment exclusively: FI and AI bodies with motor drive; lenses: 24mm f/2, 35mm f/2, 50mm f/1.4, 85mm f/1.8, 135mm f/2, 200mm f/2.8, and 300mm f/4 Aspherical, and Canon strobe system.

Peter Goddard is the rock and jazz critic for the *Toronto Star.* He has written for a variety of magazines in Canada, the U.S., and France, and recently won a National Newspaper Award for critical writing. Goddard has an M.A. in music and a degree in solo piano performance. He has written several scores for experimental film, including electronic music, and has written and produced for television and radio. Peter, his wife and daughter reside in Toronto, and they spend part of the year on their farm in France.

Goddard's first book was on Frank Sinatra, and he co-authored *The Rolling Stones Live* with photographer Philip Kamin. He is currently working on a novel.

LOUISVILLE